## TABLE OF CONTENTS

Synopsis . . . . . . . . . . . . . . . . . . . . . . . . . . . . . . . . . 1

About the Author / Background Information . . . . . . . 2

Pre-Reading Activities . . . . . . . . . . . . . . . . . . . . . . 3

Chapters I, II . . . . . . . . . . . . . . . . . . . . . . . . 4 - 7

Chapters III, IV . . . . . . . . . . . . . . . . . . . . . 8 - 10

Chapters V, VI . . . . . . . . . . . . . . . . . . . . . 11 - 13

Chapters VII, VIII . . . . . . . . . . . . . . . . . . . 14 - 15

Chapters IX, X . . . . . . . . . . . . . . . . . . . . . 16 - 18

Cloze Activity . . . . . . . . . . . . . . . . . . . . . . . . 19

Post-Reading Activities . . . . . . . . . . . . . . . . . 20 - 21

Suggestions For Further Reading . . . . . . . . . . . . . 22

Answer Key . . . . . . . . . . . . . . . . . . . . . . . . 23 - 24

*Novel-Ties® are printed on recycled paper.*

Copyright © 1983, 1999, 2007 by LEARNING LINKS

## For the Teacher

This reproducible study guide to use in conjunction with the novel *Animal Farm* consists of lessons for guided reading. Written in chapter-by-chapter format, the guide contains a synopsis, pre-reading activities, vocabulary and comprehension exercises, as well as extension activities to be used as follow-up to the novel.

In a homogeneous classroom, whole class instruction with one title is appropriate. In a heterogeneous classroom, reading groups should be formed: each group works on a different novel at its own reading level. Depending upon the length of time devoted to reading in the classroom, each novel, with its guide and accompanying lessons, may be completed in three to six weeks.

Begin using NOVEL-TIES for reading development by distributing the novel and a folder to each student. Distribute duplicated pages of the study guide for students to place in their folders. After examining the cover and glancing through the book, students can participate in several pre-reading activities. Vocabulary questions should be considered prior to reading a chapter; all other work should be done after the chapter has been read. Comprehension questions can be answered orally or in writing. The classroom teacher should determine the amount of work to be assigned, always keeping in mind that readers must be nurtured and that the ultimate goal is encouraging students' love of reading.

The benefits of using NOVEL-TIES are numerous. Students read good literature in the original, rather than in abridged or edited form. The good reading habits, formed by practice in focusing on interpretive comprehension and literary techniques, will be transferred to the books students read independently. Passive readers become active, avid readers.

## SYNOPSIS

*Animal Farm* is an allegorical tale by George Orwell in which animals attempt to create a revolutionary utopia that ultimately reverts to a more evil system than the one it replaced.

One evening on Manor Farm, after the drunken farmer Mr. Jones has gone to bed, old Major shares a vision with the other animals. Old Major is a prize Middle White boar, a highly regarded member of the animal community on the farm. As he speaks, he recalls the cruelty that humans have perpetrated against the animals on the farm, and he stirs them into thoughts of a future rebellion. Three nights later, Old Major dies, but he leaves behind his dogma, "Whatever goes upon two legs is an enemy," as well as a stirring song of rebellion titled "Beasts of England."

The pigs on the farm, thought to be the cleverest of the animals, then take over preparations for the future rebellion. Two young boars named Snowball and Napoleon lead the preparations. With the help of a brilliant talker named Squealer, they formulate a system of thought called "Animalism."

The rebellion occurs sooner than anyone expects. One night the neglectful Mr. Jones and his men forget to feed the animals. The starving animals break into the storage shed, and when Mr. Jones and his men try to beat them away from the food, they attack the humans and drive them off the farm.

In control of their lives at last, the animals make plans for improving their destiny. At first, they seem to succeed. They change the name of the farm to "Animal Farm" and paint the seven commandments of their community on the wall of the barn. A successful harvest and another victory over the humans seem to confirm their success. Then the feasibility of building a windmill sets Napoleon and Snowball against each other. Wielding the tools of subversive thought and propaganda, Napoleon convinces the other animals that Snowball is the enemy, and Snowball is expelled from the farm. Napoleon then announces that the pigs will begin to assign all the work on the farm, and the other animals will simply follow orders.

Soon all the animals become completely dominated by the pigs. Led by Napoleon, the pigs become the elite class on the farm. They conduct campaigns against various factions of the human community and form alliances with other factions for political gain. They ban the singing of "The Beasts of England," and they even alter the seven commandments written on the barn wall to reinforce and substantiate their actions. Eventually, Napoleon, seeking to tighten his control, conducts a purge of all dissidents within the farm population. The animals watch in horror and confused resignation as their friends and comrades are killed off for the "good" of the community.

Finally, the pigs become the enemies they once hated. They begin to drink excessively and walk on their hind legs. In the final scene, they give a party for the neighboring farmers in which they announce that the name of the farm will once again be Manor Farm. As they drink, gamble, and argue with their guests, the pigs become truly indistinguishable from humans. The tale has come full circle.

## ABOUT THE AUTHOR

Born Eric Blair in Bengal, India in 1903, George Orwell was educated at Eton School in London and served in the Imperial Police in Burma in the 1920s. After his assignment in Burma and a two-year stay in Paris, he returned to England and a series of jobs, including that of school teacher. He fought in the Spanish Civil War in 1936-37 and worked as an overseas broadcaster during World War II.

Orwell had dreamed of becoming a writer from a very early age, and although he attempted to abandon that idea as a young man, he found that writing was his true calling. His first book, *Down and Out in Paris and London*, was published in 1933 under his pen name George Orwell. He went on to publish numerous novels, essays, and articles. *Animal Farm*, the first book in which he used his artistic abilities to reflect a political view, was published in 1945. His novel *1984*, a chilling view of the political future, was published in 1949. Orwell died of tuberculosis in London, England on January 21, 1950.

## BACKGROUND INFORMATION

In the Communist Revolution, which took place in Russia near the end of World War I, on November 7, 1917, the Bolsheviks ousted the czar and seized control over the Congress of Soviets. The "Council of People's Commissars" with Vladimir Lenin as Chairman, Leon Trotsky as Commissar of Foreign Affairs, and Joseph Stalin as Commissar of Nationalities, formed the ruling body together with a Central Executive Committee.

As World War I was coming to an end, Lenin negotiated a peace with Germany. In 1918, in the Treaty of Brest-Litovsky, Russia granted independence to Poland, Finland, Lithuania, Latvia, and Estonia. Ukraine was added to Germany, and Turkey received parts of the Caucasus. Germany also received indemnities of grain and other produce. The White Bolsheviks, a group of Russian soldiers opposing the Red Bolsheviks in power, instigated civil war. Trotsky overcame the opposition and crushed the White army forces. Peace was restored in Russia in 1921.

After Lenin's death in 1924, Trotsky and Stalin developed opposing ideologies. Trotsky believed that the revolution in Russia could succeed only with the help of other revolutions throughout Europe. Socialism, he believed, could not survive against the industrial states of Europe. Stalin, on the other hand, believed that the revolution in Russia should be strengthened from within to ward off any attack from the hostile world outside. Trotsky believed that a strong Russia should be built upon an industry of production of consumable goods: food, clothing, and household items. Stalin believed that heavy industry, such as machinery, transportation equipment, and weapons, would keep the revolution secure. Stalin and his followers in the Communist Party voted out Trotsky, expelled him from the party, and forced him into exile. In 1929, Stalin became the Supreme Head of the Soviet Union, beginning an era of increasing central control and authoritarian government. Civil rights were disregarded, dissenting voices were silenced, artistic expression was censored, and one wave of purges followed another.

# PRE-READING ACTIVITIES

1. Preview the book by reading the title and the author's name and by looking at the illustration on the cover. Are you familiar with any other works by the same author? What do you think this book will be about?

2. **Cooperative Learning Activity:** Work with a small group to do some research on one of the forms of political thought listed below. Take notes on what you find out about this form of government, differentiating between its ideal and its practical reality in history. Share your findings with your class. As an entire class, discuss the similarities between dictatorships of the Right and those of the Left.

   - totalitarianism
   - socialism
   - communism
   - democracy

3. **Social Studies Connection:** Read the Background Information on page two of this study guide and do some additional research on the Russian Revolution and the Soviet era. Prepare a time line of the major events of the Russian Revolution of 1917 and its aftermath, up through the Stalinist purges of the 1930s. Then as you read *Animal Farm*, compare events from the novel to events in Russian history. In what ways are events similar? In what ways are they different?

4. Write a thumbnail biography of each of the following historical figures. Then as you read the novel, observe the parallels between these historical figures and fictional characters in the book.

   - Karl Marx
   - Vladimir Lenin
   - Leon Trotsky
   - Joseph Stalin

5. Conduct a round-table discussion focused on the nineteenth century historian Lord John Dalberg-Acton's quotation, "power tends to corrupt, and absolute power corrupts absolutely." Discuss how this concept can be true in interpersonal relationships among friends, in school situations, and at local and national government levels. What happens in each relationship when there is no check to absolute authority? What constitutional checks exist within our own government to limit absolute power? In your opinion, are these checks sufficient?

6. Throughout our culture there are examples of animal traits being attributed to humans, such as in the following similes:

   - as sly as a fox
   - as stubborn as a mule

   What characteristics are usually attributed to pigs, horses, sheep, and chickens? As you read the novel, notice the traits Orwell ascribes to the characters who populate Animal Farm. Do you think the personalities of these characters are consistent with the stereotypes associated with these types of animals?

7. Consult a dictionary to find the definitions of "allegory" and "fable." As you read, determine how *Animal Farm* conforms to and differs from the definitions of an allegory and a fable.

## CHAPTERS I, II

**Vocabulary:** Use the context to help you determine the meaning of the underlined word in each of the following sentences. Then write the letter of the correct meaning for each word below.

• The farmer kept sacks of potatoes and barrels of cider in the <u>scullery</u>.

• The two <u>comrades</u> looked out for each other's welfare during the revolution.

• All our belongings have arrived, and we are happily <u>ensconced</u> in our new home.

• A verdict could not be pronounced until the two <u>dissentients</u> on the jury agreed with the opinion of the others.

• The mutual <u>enmity</u> of the two nations led them to wage war on each other.

• <u>Pre-eminent</u> among the group of army officers was an old general who had fought in many battles.

• The <u>vivacious</u> child loved to laugh and play with others.

• When we climbed the <u>knoll</u> in the pasture, we could look down upon the farm house and the barn.

• The frisky young lambs <u>gambolled</u> playfully through the field.

• Wild berry bushes grew below the young trees in the <u>spinney</u>.


_____ 1. scullery   a. active hatred or ill-will

_____ 2. comrades   b. those differing in opinion

_____ 3. ensconced   c. playfully skipped about

_____ 4. dissentients   d. of the highest rank of importance

_____ 5. enmity   e. room for storing food supplies

_____ 6. pre-eminent   f. small wooded area with underbrush

_____ 7. vivacious   g. small round hill; mound

_____ 8. knoll   h. settled comfortably

_____ 9. gambolled   i. lively in actions and conduct

_____ 10. spinney   j. fellow soldiers; close companions

## Chapters I, II (cont.)

**Language Study: Multiple-Meaning Words**

Read the following sentence from the novel. Circle the letter of the correct meaning for each underlined word as it is used in the sentence.

> At the last moment Mollie, the foolish, pretty white mare who <u>drew</u> Mrs. Jones' <u>trap</u>, came <u>mincing</u> daintily in, chewing at a lump of sugar.

1. drew
   a. created a likeness by making lines on paper
   b. caused to move by hauling or dragging

2. trap
   a. device used to catch or take in something
   b. light one-horse carriage with springs

3. mincing
   a. walking with small, delicate steps
   b. chopping into very small pieces

Write a new sentence for each of the words above. Use a meaning that is different from that in the sentence from the novel.

drew    _____

trap    _____

mincing _____

**Questions:**

1. In what ways do the animals in the novel act like humans? In what ways do they retain their identities as animals?

2. What is the central message in Old Major's speech in the barn?

3. According to Old Major's speech, under what principles should the farm operate?

4. What does Snowball mean when he says to Mollie, "Those ribbons that you are devoted to are the badge of slavery"?

5. What happens during and after the rebellion?

6. What notion about the basic nature of humanity is implicit in the seven commandments drawn up for Animal Farm?

## Chapters I, II (cont.)

**Questions for Discussion:**

1.  Do you agree with Major's pronouncement that "Man is the only creature that consumes without producing"?

2.  Why do you think the other animals are so easily led by the pigs? Would you have been so willing to follow another leader after you had freed yourself of oppression?

3.  What do you think happened to the milk that is missing?

**Compare and Contrast: Snowball and Napoleon**

Use the Venn diagram below to compare and contrast the two young boars, Snowball and Napoleon. Write their unique qualities below their names. Write the qualities that they share in the overlapping part of the circles.

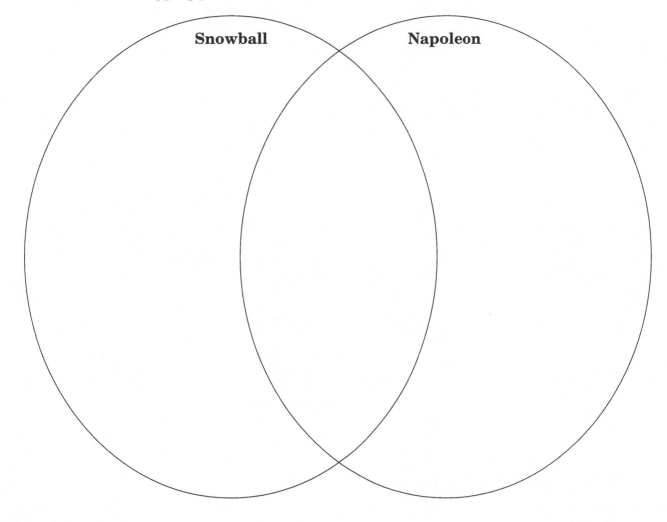

## Chapters I, II (cont.)

**Literary Device: Point of View**

Point of view in literature refers to the person telling the story. *Animal Farm* is written from the third-person point of view, with an omniscient narrator who knows about all the events that occur on the farm, as well as the thoughts and feelings of all the characters. Why do you think Orwell chose to use the third-person point of view in the novel? How does the third-person point of view help you understand the novel? What might be its shortcomings?

_____

_____

_____

_____

_____

**Writing Activity:**

Describe the events in the first two chapters from the point of view of one of the animals on the farm.

## CHAPTERS III, IV

**Vocabulary:** Synonyms are words with similar meanings. Read the sentences below and circle the letter of the best synonym for each underlined word.

1. The hungry man found <u>acute</u> pleasure in sampling the many tasty dishes presented by his host.

   a. painful      b. mild      c. intense      d. absurd

2. The <u>obstinate</u> worker complained whenever his everyday routine was interrupted in any way.

   a. diligent      b. lazy      c. inflexible      d. cooperative

3. My friend left such <u>cryptic</u> travel directions on my answering machine that I got lost.

   a. puzzling      b. deadly      c. obvious      d. interesting

4. Because we believed in the ideas of the political candidate, we were <u>indefatigable</u> in promoting his cause.

   a. tragic      b. unflagging      c. halfhearted      d. slow

5. The store owner was <u>shrewd</u> in her dealings with customers, making a very good profit.

   a. dim-witted      b. cruel      c. calculating      d. polite

6. Because of their gentle nature, the <u>tractable</u> cows were easy to herd in and out of the barn.

   a. vicious      b. submissive      c. stubborn      d. dappled

7. The young child's laughter was <u>irrepressible</u>, and even his mother could not quiet him.

   a. delightful      b. controlled      c. unrestrained      d. hushed

8. The would-be burglar fled in <u>ignominious</u> retreat as he saw a police car turning the corner.

   a. honorable      b. casual      c. astonished      d. shameful

## Chapters III, IV (cont.)

### Questions:

1. In what ways are the animals of Animal Farm building a new society?

2. Describe the flag that Snowball designs for the farm. What is the significance of the color of the flag and the symbols on it?

3. What evidence shows that Napoleon and Snowball are beginning to compete for power?

4. What maxim does Snowball use to simplify the Seven Commandments? Why is this maxim a good propaganda technique?

5. In what ways do the pigs set themselves up as the elite members of Animal Farm?

6. What part does Squealer play in the brainwashing of the animals?

7. In what ways do the animals perform like a disciplined army in the Battle of the Cowshed? How is this battle different from the Rebellion?

8. Why are Snowball and Boxer decorated? How does each feel about his success?

### Questions for Discussion:

1. If you could be any one of the animals in the novel, which animal would you choose to be?

2. Why do you think Napoleon decided to educate the young puppies in seclusion? What purpose might this isolation serve? What might be the outcome of the puppies' education?

### Writing Acitivty: A Newspaper Story

Imagine that you are a reporter for a newspaper near Animal Farm. Write an article about the Battle of the Cowshed. Make your story as impartial as possible, reporting facts and avoiding editorial comments. Remember, a good newspaper story answers the questions: *Who? What? Where? When? How?* and *Why?*

# Chapters III, IV (cont.)

## Literary Device: Symbolism

Symbolism in literature refers to simple ideas, objects, or events that represent complex sets of ideas. In the chart below indicate what each element from the novel might symbolize.

| Object/Idea | Symbol |
|---|---|
| 1. The song, "Beasts of England" | |
| 2. Sugarcandy Mountain | |
| 3. The whips of Mr. Jones and his men | |
| 4. The horses' ribbons | |
| 5. The Seven Commandments | |
| 6. The milk and the windfall apples | |
| 7. The Battle of the Cowshed | |

## CHAPTERS V, VI

**Vocabulary:** Analogies are word equations in which the first pair of words has the same relationship as the second pair of words. For example: DAWN is to DUSK as JOYOUS is to SAD. Both pairs of words are opposites. Choose the best word from the Word Box to complete each of the following analogies.

| WORD BOX | | | |
|---|---|---|---|
| arable | canvassing | quarry | silage |
| abolished | innovations | restive | |

1. PROCURING is to ACQUIRING as _____ is to SOLICITING.

2. TRADITIONS is to OLD as _____ is to NEW.

3. FEED is to _____ as GENERATOR is to DYNAMO.

4. REASONABLE is to EXTRAVAGANT as BARREN is to _____.

5. _____ is to IMPATIENT as CONTROVERSY is to DISAGREEMENT.

6. WATER is to WELL as STONE is to _____.

7. EXPELLED is to WELCOMED as _____ is to RESTORED.

**Questions:**

1. Why does Mollie leave the farm? How do the other animals react to her leaving?

2. In what way does the idea of building a windmill serve to deepen the animosity between Snowball and Napoleon?

3. How does Napoleon overthrow Snowball?

4. After Napoleon takes control of the farm, how does life for the animals compare to the life that they led under Mr. Jones?

5. What argument does Squealer use to keep the animals from protesting Napoleon's takeover? In what way is this argument valuable as propaganda?

## Chapters V, VI (cont.)

6. Because Boxer believes that "Napoleon is always right," his personal motto becomes, "I will work harder." What does this reveal about Boxer's character?

7. How does Napoleon take credit for the construction of the windmill?

8. In what ways does Napoleon bend the rules and commandments of Animal Farm to benefit himself?

9. How does Napoleon use Snowball as a scapegoat when the windmill is blown down?

**Questions for Discussion:**

1. Consider the way in which Napoleon bends the truth and manipulates others in order to ensure his ultimate power and control. How do his words and actions exemplify the concept, "Power corrupts"?

2. In your opinion, how would the events at Animal Farm be different if Snowball had assumed the leadership and Napoleon had been exiled?

**Literary Devices:**

I. *Irony*—When dramatic irony is used in a work of literature, readers are given an insight into situations that the characters do not have. With this device, the characters often believe one thing to be true, while the readers know it is not. What is ironic in Squealer's following statement to the animals:

> Do not imagine comrades that leadership is a pleasure! On the contrary, it is a deep and heavy responsibility. No one believes more firmly than Comrade Napoleon that all animals are equal. He would be only too happy to let you make decisions for yourselves. But sometimes you might make the wrong decision, comrades, and then where would we be?

_____

_____

_____

_____

## Chapters V, VI (cont.)

II. *Euphemism*—A euphemism is an agreeable expression that is substituted for an unpleasant or offensive word. For example, Squealer uses the word "tactics" as a euphemism for "manipulation" when he refers to Napoleon's plan to rid the farm of Snowball.

- What is the literal meaning of the word "tactics"?

_____

_____

- What is the literal meaning of the word "manipulation"?

_____

_____

- Why do you think Squealer uses the word "tactics" instead of "manipulation" when he speaks to the animals?

_____

_____

Find other examples of euphemism as you continue to read the novel.

### Writing Activity: Propaganda

Propaganda can be defined as ideas, information, or allegations spread deliberately to further one's cause or to harm an opposing cause. Propaganda is used to influence the thinking of others. It can be found in print and speech, as well as on radio and television. Many advertisements use elements of propaganda to make items seem desirable to buyers. Use an encyclopedia to do some research on various techniques of propaganda. Then write an advertisement in which you try to influence the emotions of others in order to persuade them to buy a product such as toothpaste, jeans, or a soft drink. Read your advertisement aloud to a group of classmates. Can they identify the elements of propaganda in the advertisement that you wrote?

## CHAPTERS VII, VIII

**Vocabulary:** Antonyms are words with opposite meanings. Draw a line from each word in column A to its antonym in column B. Then use the words in column A to fill in the blanks in the sentences below.

|   | A |   |   | B |
|---|---|---|---|---|
| 1. | capitulated | | a. | forgiveness |
| 2. | tumult | | b. | irreverently |
| 3. | retribution | | c. | jubilation |
| 4. | nocturnal | | d. | hostile |
| 5. | beatifically | | e. | resisted |
| 6. | conciliatory | | f. | sophisticated |
| 7. | lamentation | | g. | serenity |
| 8. | primitive | | h. | daytime |

. . . . . . . . . . . . . . . . . . . . . . . . . . . . . . . . . . . . . . . . . . . . . .

1. Having only _____ tools at our disposal, we could build nothing more than a simple shed as a shelter.

2. I wrote a _____ letter to my friend, apologizing for the argument we had last week.

3. In the _____ after the meeting, people jumped out of their seats and shouted at each other.

4. The criminals finally _____ when their supply of food and water gave out after a three-day siege.

5. We took a _____ walk through the woods, using flashlights and the glow of the full moon to light our way.

6. The people of the community sent up a cry of _____ when they saw how the wildfires had destroyed their homes.

7. The woman smiled _____ at her children as they joined her in saying a short prayer before dinner.

8. The vandals suffered the _____ of the townspeople when they were made to pay for what they destroyed.

### Questions:

1. What techniques does Napoleon use to make it appear to the outside world that everything is going well at Animal Farm, even though the economy of the farm is about to collapse?

2. What happens to the hens when they threaten Napoleon's power?

## Chapters VII, VIII (cont.)

3. How does Napoleon use the memory of the absent Snowball to keep the animals in line?

4. Why does Clover sing "Beasts of England" after the rash of executions? What does this reveal about Clover's character?

5. What reason does Napoleon give the other animals for abolishing the song "Beasts of England"? What is Napoleon's real reason for banning the song?

6. What evidence at the beginning of Chapter Eight shows that Napoleon is systematically lying to the other animals?

7. What clues suggest that Napoleon is becoming more and more like a human?

8. How do the animals feel about the Battle of the Windmill? How have their beliefs been manipulated?

### Questions for Discussion:

1. How does the poem entitled "Comrade Napoleon" enhance Napoleon's image? What emotions does the poem elicit from the reader?

2. In what ways does Napoleon set himself up as a demigod, a person who has or thinks he has powers that are almost divine? What is the significance of the purge in which Napoleon executes four pigs?

### Literary Device: Irony

Irony refers to the use of a word or phrase to mean the exact opposite of its literal or normal meaning. In general discussion, to be human or humane suggests the qualities of compassion and kindness. What ironic comment does the author make when he suggests that Napoleon is becoming more human?

_____

_____

_____

### Writing Activity:

What do you think will happen to the animals on the farm in the future? Think about all that has occurred so far. Consider what you know about political revolutions that have occurred in recent history. Based on clues from the story and your own knowledge, write a brief summary describing how the novel might end. Compare your predictions to those of your classmates. Then continue to read the novel to check the predictions you made.

# CHAPTERS IX, X

**Vocabulary:** Draw a line from each word or phrase on the left to its definition on the right. Then use the numbered words to fill in the blanks in the sentences below.

| | | | |
|---|---|---|---|
| 1. | poultices | a. | clever remarks |
| 2. | superannuated | b. | relating to a child or offspring |
| 3. | gill | c. | in a way that is sparing, not wasteful |
| 4. | rheumy | d. | viciously evil or harmful |
| 5. | filial | e. | measure of fluid capacity, about four ounces |
| 6. | frugally | f. | retired because of age or infirmity |
| 7. | *bon mots* | g. | medicated materials that are spread on sores |
| 8. | malignant | h. | watery |

. . . . . . . . . . . . . . . . . . . . . . . . . . . . . . . . . . . . . . . . . . . . .

1. A corner of the kennel was set aside for _____ guard dogs who could no longer protect their masters.

2. The guests at the dinner applauded and laughed aloud at the master of ceremony's _____.

3. Only a(n) _____ of beer was offered to the young man.

4. We were led to believe that we would be attacked by some _____ enemy.

5. If you wish to save money for the future, you must live _____.

6. Without access to doctors, they used old-fashioned _____ to soothe the pain of burns.

7. Fulfilling my _____ responsibility, I offered my father assistance in all of our home repair chores.

8. Hampered by _____ eyes and a slow gait, the old race horse was put out to pasture.

## Chapters IX, X (cont.)

**Questions:**

1. In what ways has Squealer become a master at explaining the shifts in Napoleon's policies?

2. What purpose does Napoleon cite as the reason for the weekly Spontaneous Demonstrations? What is their real purpose?

3. Why do you think Moses was allowed to return and remain on the farm?

4. Why do the animals on the farm admire Boxer? What are the details of Boxer's demise?

5. Animal Farm has become a stratified society with two classes. What are those two classes?

6. How has Napoleon become indistinguishable from Mr. Jones?

7. Napoleon is praised by the neighboring farmers for increasing production while providing less food for his laborers. Why is this praise ironic?

8. What began as a paradise for the animals has now ended as the antithesis of Utopia. Describe the scene at the end of the book when the transformation from pig to human is complete. What is the new name for Animal Farm?

**Questions for Discussion:**

1. Elitism is leadership by a socially superior minority group. In what ways is elitism fostered among the pigs of Animal Farm? Do you think they are justified in the belief that they are superior animals?

2. In your opinion, was there ever a moment in which Animal Farm might have reached a Utopian state? If so, describe the circumstances in which this could have happened. If not, give reasons for your answer.

3. George Orwell subtitled this novel, *A Fairy Story*. Why do you think Orwell chose that subtitle for *Animal Farm*? In what ways is the novel a fairy story? In what ways is it very different from conventional fairy stories? What irony is there in this subtitle?

## Chapters IX, X (cont.)

**Literary Devices:**

I. *Symbolism*

What does the windmill symbolize at the beginning of the novel, before it is built?

_____

How does the symbolism grow and change as the novel progresses?

_____

_____

How does the windmill reflect and support the political climate on the farm?

_____

_____

II. *Satire*—Satire is a literary device in which the vices and follies of characters or situations are held up to ridicule and scorn.

- In what way does Orwell use the novel to satirize extreme political views?

- How are both the leaders and the followers of Animal Farm satirized?

- What viewpoints does Orwell express through his use of satire?

**Writing Activity:**

Imagine that you are a literary critic. Write a review of the novel *Animal Farm*. In the review, tell why you liked or disliked the novel. Describe the ways in which Orwell expressed his political viewpoint through characters and events. Tell whether or not you agree with that viewpoint. Also, touch upon Orwell's simple, straight-forward writing style. Do you think it is effective in the novel?

After writing your review, work with a group of classmates to conduct a panel discussion. Appoint one member of the group as the moderator for the panel. Take turns reading your reviews and discussing them. In what ways do your opinions of the book differ? What aspects of the book do you agree upon? What is your general consensus on the book as a whole?

## CLOZE ACTIVITY

The following passage is taken from Chapter One of *Animal Farm*. Read the passage completely. Then fill in each blank with a word that makes sense. After you fill in the blanks, you may go back and compare your language with that of the author.

Man is the only creature that consumes without producing. He does not give

milk, he does not lay _____,[1] he is too weak to pull the _____,[2]

he cannot run fast enough to catch _____.[3] Yet he is lord of all the

_____.[4] He sets them to work, he gives _____[5] to them the

bare minimum that will _____[6] them from starving, and the rest he

_____[7] for himself. Our labour tills the soil, _____[8] dung fertilises

it, and yet there is _____[9] one of us that owns more than _____[1]

bare skin. You cows that I see _____[11] me, how many thousands of gallons of

_____[12] have you given during this last year? _____[13] what has

happened to that milk which _____[14] have been breeding up sturdy calves?

Every _____[15] of it has gone down the throats _____[16] our

enemies. And you hens, how many _____[17] have you laid in this last year,

_____[18] how many of those eggs ever hatched _____[19] chickens?

The rest have all gone to _____[20] to bring in money for Jones and

_____[21] men. And you, Clover, where are those _____[22] foals you

bore, who should have been _____[23] support and pleasure of your old age?

_____[24] was sold at a year old— you _____[25] never see one of them

again. In return for your four confinements and all your labour in the fields, what have

you ever had except your bare rations and a stall?

# POST-READING ACTIVITIES

1. Return to the time line that you began in the Pre-Reading Activities on page three of this study guide. Add further information as you compare the sequence of events that followed the Russian Revolution to the events in *Animal Farm*. Then compare your timeline with others who have read the same book.

2. With your classmates discuss how the events in *Animal Farm* are similar to events that are occurring in the world today. What lessons does the book teach that might help to solve some of these problems?

3. Return to the Venn diagram that you began on page six of this study guide in which you compared the characters of Snowball and Napolean. Add more information and compare your responses with those of your classmates.

4. The theme of a work of fiction is a system of ideas that forms an important message. In this novel, Orwell's main themes include the following:
   - Characters of good will attempt to improve their lives only to discover the old evils of pride and hypocrisy in themselves.
   - Man's inhumanity to man is often for the sake of political gain.
   - Governments can bend people to any purpose through the use of propaganda.
   - A vision of a better society can be corrupted if care and watchfulness are not exercised by its citizens.

   Add any additional statements of theme that you feel are pertinent to the novel. Then select any one of the themes and describe in writing how the novel illustrated that idea. Be as specific as possible, quoting from the novel when appropriate.

5. Work with a group of classmates to discuss the following questions:
   - Who must accept the blame for the failure of Animal Farm? Is it Snowball, Napoleon, Old Major, the pigs, the humans, or all of the animals?
   - What does Orwell want the reader to conclude about political systems?
   - Who is to blame when governments become autocratic? Is it the leader of the government, the party that granted the power, or all of the people?
   - Orwell claimed that he attempted "to fuse political purpose into one whole" in the novel *Animal Farm*. Was he successful in doing this?

6. On an allegorical level, *Animal Farm* traces the steps of the Russian Revolution. However, it has been said that Orwell was interested in tracing the path of any political revolution. Form a panel with a group of classmates. Discuss the following steps that are typical of revolutions that occurred in countries such as Russia, France, Spain, and Cuba:
   - revolution
   - period of euphoria and commitment
   - tightening of authority and sacrifices to meet goals
   - control gained by the new elite.

## Post-Reading Activities (cont.)

7. Write a brief fictional story to satirize an actual political event in modern history, such as the Joseph McCarthy hearings, Watergate, the hostage crisis in Iran, the collapse of the Soviet Union, the incursion of the Taliban in Afghanistan, or the war in Iraq. Share your satire by reading it aloud in class.

8. Using your own political convictions as a basis, create a list of seven or more "commandments" that state the ideals you feel are important for people to follow in order to have a peaceful, productive society. Post your commandments on the classroom wall along with the commandments written by your classmates. Hold a classroom discussion to explain and defend these commandments.

9. Utopian fiction can be defined as literature that presents an ideal environment for mankind in which moral ills and political injustice do not exist. Explore this concept by reading one or more of the following works of literature and reporting on them in class. Then with your classmates, discuss the ways in which *Animal Farm* can be considered to be an example of "anti-utopian" fiction.
   - Plato's *Republic*
   - *Utopia*, by Sir Thomas More
   - *New Atlantis*, by Francis Bacon
   - *Gulliver's Travels*, by Jonathan Swift
   - *Typee and Omoo*, by Herman Melville
   - *Erewhon*, by Samuel Butler
   - *A Modern Utopia*, by H. G. Wells
   - *Walden Two*, by B. F. Skinner

# SUGGESTIONS FOR FURTHER READING

\* Adams, Richard. *Watership Down*. Simon & Schuster.

      _____. *The Plague Dogs*. Random House.

  Bellamy, Edward. *Looking Backward*. New American Library.

  Boulle, Pierre. *Planet of the Apes*. Random House.

\* Bradbury, Ray. *Fahrenheit 451*. Random House

\* Cormier, Robert. *The Chocolate War*. Random House.

\* Golding, William. *Lord of the Flies*. Putnam.

  Hilton, James. *Lost Horizon*. Simon & Schuster.

  Howe, Irving, ed. *1984 Revisited: Totalitarianism in Our Century*. HarperCollins.

  Huxley, Aldous. *Brave New World*. HarperCollins.

      _____. *Brave New World Revisited*. HarperCollins.

  Kafka, Franz. *The Metamorphosis*. Random House.

\* Lowry, Lois. *The Giver*. Random House.

  Macaulay, David. *Baaa*. Houghton Mifflin.

\* Shakespeare, William. *Julius Caesar*. Penguin.

  Skinner, B. F. *Walden Two*. Simon & Schuster.

  Smyer, Richard I. *Animal Farm: Pastoralism & Politics*. Twayne.

\* Steinbeck, John. *The Pearl*. Penguin.

\* Strasser, Todd. *The Wave*. Random House.

  Swift, Jonathan. *Gulliver's Travels*. Penguin.

\* Tolkien, J. R. R. *The Hobbit*. Random House.

      _____. *Lord of the Rings*. Random House.

**Some Other Books by George Orwell**

  *Burmese Days*. Harcourt.

  *Coming Up for Air*. Harcourt.

  *Clergyman's Daughter*. Harcourt.

  *The English People*. Haskell.

  *Keep the Sapidistra Flying*. Harcourt.

\* *1984*. New American Library.

  *The Road to Wigon Pier*. Harcourt.

  *Shooting an Elephant*. Harcourt.

\* NOVEL-TIES Study Guides are available for these titles.

# ANSWER KEY

**Chapters I, II**
Vocabulary: 1. e  2. j  3. h  4. b  5. a  6. d  7. i  8. g  9. c  10. f
Language
Study: 1. b  2. b  3. a
Questions: 1. The animals think, discuss, argue, and care for each other's welfare as though they were human. They also display the typical animal behavior for each of their species. 2. Old Major encourages rebellion so that the animals can benefit from their own labor and escape the abuse of humans. 3. Major espouses four principles: all animals are equal, all creatures with two legs are enemies, all creatures with four legs are comrades, and animals must not adopt the habits of humans. 4. Snowball means that if Mollie requires material possessions, such as ribbons, she will never be free of the humans who supply them to her. 5. On a night when Mr. Jones neglected to feed the animals, they broke into the store-shed themselves. As Mr. Jones and his men tried to beat off the animals, they were attacked and run off the farm. The animals had a joyous celebration, destroying everything on the farm that reminded them of their dependence on humans. 6. All of the seven commandments suggest that humans and their ways are evil.

**Chapters III, IV**
Vocabulary: 1. c  2. c  3. a  4. b  5. c  6. b  7. c  8. d
Questions: 1. The animals act cooperatively to accomplish the work on the farm. Each animal works according to his capacity. The quarrels and jealousy of the old days are almost gone. 2. The flag is green with a hoof and a horn on it. The green color represents the green fields of England. The hoof and the horn represent the transcendence of animals over humans. 3. Evidence that Napoleon and Snowball's joint governorship is starting to fail is evident when they disagree at public meetings and criticize each other's actions. 4. Snowball uses the maxim, "Four legs good, two legs bad." This is a simple slogan that even the dim-witted animals can remember, and the sheep begin to chant it aloud. 5. The pigs make themselves the leaders of the animals and take the best food in the greatest quantity. 6. Squealer convinces the animals that the pigs really need the apples and milk that they receive to help them manage the farm. 7. The animals are organized for this battle and form strike teams. They maneuver the humans into an ambush. The original rebellion was spontaneous and, therefore, chaotic. 8. Snowball and Boxer are decorated for their effectiveness in battle. Boxer is sad that he killed a boy, while Snowball is pleased with the success of the battle and will not permit any sentimentality.

**Chapters V, VI**
Vocabulary: 1. canvassing  2. innovations  3. silage  4. arable  5. restive  6. quarry  7. abolished
Questions: 1. Mollie leaves the farm because she prefers to be a pampered pet of humans rather than toil for an independent life on the farm. She runs away to a human, and the other animals never mention her again. 2. Snowball believes that the windmill will be a great labor-saving device. Napoleon, who has no innovative schemes of his own, says the idea will not work and wants the animals to concentrate on food production. 3. Napoleon overthrows Snowball by resorting to force, running Snowball off the farm with attack dogs—the dogs that Napoleon had reared privately as puppies. 4. With his dogs to help him enforce his power, Napoleon replaces Jones as an oppressor. As Jones once did, Napoleon now takes on absolute power and permits no one to question his authority. 5. Squealer says that Napoleon recognizes that all animals are equal, but feels that he must assume leadership because the animals are unable to make their own decisions. In this way, the animals are persuaded to feel grateful for the opportunity to hand over their power to an absolute leader. 6. Boxer is good hearted and a hard worker, but he is a true follower. He is not bright and cannot perceive the true meaning of the events that are going on around him. 7. Napoleon, now appreciating the value of the windmill, tells the animals that it was his plan all along. 8. Napoleon changes the Seven Commandments to make his actions seem acceptable. He blames Snowball for initiating lies that oppose his actions. 9. Using Snowball as a scapegoat, Napoleon says that Snowball is responsible for the "overthrow" of the windmill. He uses the emotion of this declaration to rally the animals and convince them that the windmill must be rebuilt.

**Chapters VII, VIII**
Vocabulary: 1. e  2. g  3. a  4. h  5. b  6. d  7. c  8. f; 1. primitive  2. conciliatory  3. tumult  4. capitulated  5. nocturnal  6. lamentation  7. beatifically  8. retribution
Questions: 1. To make things appear as if the farm is prospering, Napoleon fills the food bins with sand and covers the tops with the little bit of produce that remains. When Mr. Whymper makes his visit, the bins appear to be full, and some of the animals are instructed to talk about how their rations

have been increased. 2. When the hens threaten Napoleon's power, their food ration is eliminated. The hens hold out for five days. Then they go back to their nesting. Nine hens die during this protest. 3. Using the memory of Snowball to keep the animals in line, Napoleon forces rebellious animals to admit to crimes that they supposedly perpetrated in collaboration with Snowball. Then Napoleon executes them. 4. Clover is so inherently good that she cannot accept evil in others. The song is her statement of faith in the revolution. 5. Napoleon tells the animals that the revolution is now completed and they no longer need the song. In reality, he fears the camaraderie of the song, preferring all loyalty be directed toward himself. 6. As evidence of Napoleon's lying, the Seven Commandments continue to be subtly changed. The words "without cause" have been tagged onto the commandment "No animal shall kill any other animal." 7. Napoleon reveals that he is becoming more human when he inhabits separate apartments from the others, has dogs to act as servants, eats his meals on fine china, and drinks alcohol. 8. The animals are depressed about the cost in lives at the Battle of the Windmill until Squealer uses propaganda techniques to make the event seem like a brilliant victory.

**Chapters IX, X**

Vocabulary: 1. g  2. f  3. e  4. h  5. b  6. c  7. a  8. d; 1. superannuated  2. *bon mots*  3. gill  4. malignant  5. frugally  6. poultices  7. filial  8. rheumy

Questions: 1. Students may cite any examples in which Squealer uses propaganda to glorify Napoleon and justify his actions. 2. Napoleon says the demonstrations are to celebrate the victories and triumphs of the farm. In reality, the purpose of the demonstrations is to make the animals forget about the hardships and shortages on the farm. 3. Moses was allowed to return because his stories helped the other animals endure their difficulties. 4. The animals admire Boxer for his kindness and dedication to hard work. When Boxer falls ill, he is taken away to be slaughtered. The animals are told that he was taken to a veterinary surgeon and that he died in a hospital. 5. The pigs represent the upper class, with the dogs as their enforcers. All of the other animals are the proletariat, or lower class. 6. It is obvious that Napoleon is becoming more and more like Mr. Jones because he walks on two legs, wears Mr. Jones' clothes, and smokes a pipe. 7. It is ironic that the success of Animal Farm is based on the standards that had once been the cause of the rebellion. 8. Students should cite the ways in which the pigs have become physically indistinguishable from humans. Animal Farm has reverted to its original name, Manor Farm.